ATTILA JÓZSEF
SELECTED
POEMS

ATTILA JÓZSEF SELECTED POEMS

Translation by Peter Hargitai

iUniverse, Inc.
New York Lincoln Shanghai

Attila József Selected Poems

Copyright © 2005 by Peter Hargitai

All rights reserved. No part of this book may be used or reproduced by any means, graphic, electronic, or mechanical, including photocopying, recording, taping or by any information storage retrieval system without the written permission of the publisher except in the case of brief quotations embodied in critical articles and reviews.

iUniverse books may be ordered through booksellers or by contacting:

iUniverse
2021 Pine Lake Road, Suite 100
Lincoln, NE 68512
www.iuniverse.com
1-800-Authors (1-800-288-4677)

ISBN-13: 978-0-595-35614-0 (pbk)
ISBN-13: 978-0-595-67246-2 (cloth)
ISBN-13: 978-0-595-80094-0 (ebk)
ISBN-10: 0-595-35614-1 (pbk)
ISBN-10: 0-595-67246-9 (cloth)
ISBN-10: 0-595-80094-7 (ebk)

Printed in the United States of America

Acknowledgements

Apalachee Quarterly: "Bitter," "Nothing," "Young Lobster, Red Lobster"; *Blue Unicorn*: "Mamma"; *Forum: Ten Poets of the Western Reserve:* "Stones"; *Palmetto Review*: "A Transparent Lion," "The Bellman of the Lake's Tower," "Drunk on the Tracks," "Sorrow," "Look"; *Prairie Schooner*: "Weary Man"; *Sands*: "Eagle," "Paris," "Smoke," "Diamonds"; *Translation Review*: "I Am Not the One Shouting." Some of the poems previously published in the book *Perched On Nothing's Branch* by Apalachee Press in 1986, 1987, 1989 and 1993, and by White Pine Press in 1999, appear in these selected poems in altered form.

The publication of this book was made possible, in part, by the FIG Program of Florida International University.

for Mancika

Contents

ONE: SON OF EARTH AND OIL

Hungary is Far Away	3
Elegy	5
Winter Night	8
Glassmakers	12
The Final Battle	13
By the Danube	15
Welcoming Thomas Mann	19
Woodcutter	21
On the City's Edge	22
Fire!	26
Ode	28
Hang On!	34
Air!	35
The Dog	38
Night in the Ghetto	39
I AM NOT THE ONE SHOUTING	43
The Eagle	44
The Last Warrior	45

TWO: SONS AND LOVERS

Mamma	49
Too Late for a Eulogy	50
My Mother Just Died	52

Strength Song	53
Autumn	54
Without Knocking	55
Biblical	56
Rising at Dawn Like the Bakers	58
Kiszombor Song	60
For Mancika	61
You're Such a Fool	62
Judit	64
Spring Mud	65
Insects	66
Sleep Silently	67
Night	68
You Made Me a Child	70
The Secrets of the Heart	72
My Love	74
Sacrilege	75
I Wait For You	76

THREE: SON OF MAN

The Lord is High	79
Young Lobster, Red Lobster	80
Dance of Flames	81
Moonlight	83
Unloading Lumber	85
Bethlehem	86
Spring Suddenly From the Tide	87
I'm Serious	88
Attila József	90
About a Poet	91
Sometimes Islands	92

Now I See	*93*
Nesting in the Forest	*95*
The Man Spoke	*96*

FOUR: PERCHED ON NOTHING'S BRANCH

A Tree Here, a Tree There	*99*
With all My Heart	*101*
On My Birthday	*102*
Sit, Stand, Kill, and Die	*104*
You Come With a Stick	*106*
Monument on a Mountaintop	*108*
Medallions	*109*
Paris	*114*
Stones	*115*
Everything Is Old	*117*
My Net	*118*
Leaves on a Tree	*119*
Diamonds	*120*
Yellow Grass	*121*
Look	*122*
Soapy Water	*123*
Sorrow	*124*
I May Just Vanish	*125*
The Sky Is Ablaze	*126*
Consciousness	*127*
Smoke	*131*
Bitter	*132*
I Threw It	*133*
The Ant	*134*
Rain	*135*

I'm Leaving Everything   *136*
Perched on Nothing's Branch   *138*

FIVE: AT THE SAND'S WET EDGE

Bathing in the Sea   *143*
Shadows   *144*
Longing Under the Moon   *145*
The Bellman of the Lake's Tower   *146*
Hearsay   *147*
My Funeral   *148*
Balatonszárszó   *149*
On Glasses   *151*
Summoning the Lion   *152*
A Transparent Lion   *154*
The Smoke   *155*
It's Only the Sea   *156*
Freight Trains   *157*
A Summer Afternoon   *158*
Autumn Dusk   *159*
Loneliness   *160*
Drunk on the Tracks   *161*
Nothing   *162*
Weary Man   *163*
Dew   *164*

About Attila József   165

About the Translator   169

ONE
Son of Earth and Oil

Hungary is Far Away

Hungary is far away.
Hungary is beyond the mountains.
She comes only when blackbirds sing,
she comes wearing next to nothing,
she comes at dawn
in light,
when the wind is warmer.
I hear her clear song,
I hear the anvil and the hammer.

Lord, have you seen Hungary?
I know her tongue is not easy.
I know my heart is heavy.
Lord, have you seen Hungary?

Girls are running
like the morning wind,
their hair chases clouds
in the eastern sky.
And here she is
braiding bread.
Oh, she is more slender
than the scent of this lily,
more threadbare than its
night shadow.

Lord, have you seen Hungary?
It is autumn there.

Lord, have you forgotten where
you could've planted her?
Your dry, rustling, lonely flower?

Elegy

Under bloated leaden skies
smoke floats above the landscape
as my soul, hovering low,
too heavy to soar.
Hardened spirit, delicate images,
follow the truth of the ages,
footprints toward the self,
toward the source. Look below

to another time
when you hunkered under
tumultuous skies
by haggard bulkheads
by the silence of anguish,
foreboding, pleading,
dissolving the thickness
of gloom in the mingling
of millions.

A whole race
is molded here. Everything in ruins.
The stiff dandelion opens its parasol
in the blight of foundry yards.
Through broken shards
the day ascends its sallow stairs
in sodden light.

Answer me.
Are you also from here?

Where the fierce longing
never ends.
A wretched sage,
squeezed by his enormous age,
the visage distorted in every face,
in every word, in every line.

Rest here. Where crippled borders
creak and groan,
keep vigil over a priggish order.
Recognize yourself? We wait
in the empty space
for a future that is solid, lovely
as plots dreaming tall houses
weaving the noise of life.

Only shards
wedged in mud cracks
can look at the grass
with those marble eyes.

A thimbleful of sand
is sprayed from the dunes. Drone.
Green and black flies swarm
for man's scraps and the rag.
A table is set
on a mortgaged plot of earth.
Yellow grass blooms in iron spittoons.

Recognize it?
The desolate joy

that keeps drawing you back
to a landscape that won't
let you go? The exquisite
suffering that keeps you there?
A child beaten
into a faraway corner
longing for his mother?
A place where you can cry?
Where you can bear to be yourself?
Where you can bear to be alone?
My God, my God, this is my home.

Winter Night

Steel yourself!

Summer's blaze
has flickered out.
Embers glow
above burnt heaps.
The country is quiet,
the air's
fine glass
is scratched by thickets.
Lovely inhumanity. A thin strip
of sliver cloth—some kind of ribbon—
hangs desperately on
a branch.
The only smile
on these knotty boughs.

In the distance
gnarled mountains like heavy hands
hold the dying light,
the smoking village,
the sighing moss,
the round silence of the valleys.

A peasant plods home to his hovel,
his joints stare blankly at the soil,
a cracked shovel hobbles on his shoulder;
the handle bleeds, the iron bleeds,
the legs grow heavier, the shovel heavier,

he barely keeps body and soul together.

Night ascends with sparkling stars
like smoke from a chimney.

A church bell
clangs the steel-blue night,
and the heart is still, and something else,
the living land
beats on, the winter night, the winter sky,
the winter ore
is the bell
and its tongue is the earth, the forged and
heavy earth,
and the heart is the voice.

The intellect weighs the memory of sounds:
winter hammering, ironing
a patch of sky,
wheat billowing wind,
light and hay falling
all summer long.

They glitter
like the soul of thought,
this winter night.

Silence locks the earth
by forging a moon.

A raven wafts through frigid space

and the lull cools.
Bone, can you hear the lull?
The clinking of the molecules?

What cabinet can hold
such glittering nights?

A branch lifts a dagger to the frost,
the black void trembles,
crows float up and down
in the fog.

Winter night.

A freight train moves
like blocks of darkness,
smoke stars swirl and die
in infinite slices.

The light darts across boxcars
like a mouse,
the flame of this winter night.

Winter steams
above cities,
streaks into the city
on glittering rails. Blue frost,
yellow light's flame.

It makes sharp weapons of anguish
in the city,

this relentless night.

On the outskirts
streetlights fall like sodden hay.

A coat rustles,
a man huddles,
frost has bitten his foot

to the bone.

His arms are rusty branches
reaching out,
he hugs this winter night
as his own.

Glassmakers

Glassmakers start great fires,
and in their kettles mix sweat
and blood with matter until limpid.
Then they are poured into tablets,
the last drop of their strong hands
roll them smooth until perfect.
As the sun dawns over cities
and village hovels, they spread
the light. Sometimes we call them
hired hands, sometimes poets,
though there is little distinction.
Slowly they bleed all color
and become transparent, brilliant,
great crystal windows through which
they can see what is to come.

The Final Battle

I scrubbed boilers,
cut down flowers,
got sentenced,
mocked in prison
as poet, artist,
propagandist,
charlatan.
I loved a woman
who liked singing
and baking bread
for other men.
She gave them looks
and other presents.
I gave out books
to working peasants.
I made love to a rich girl
in a bind, but her kind
was less than kind.
Now I eat every other day,
my ulcer eats me every day.
As the world turns
my stomach churns,
love inside me burns,
the world is sick,
wars are bloody vomit.
Our mouths eat nothing
but cowardly silence.
I kick myself to make a difference!
I'm a poet in a chaotic age

offered plenty for his rage.
Priests say: "Work for the Lord."
The truth is I'm powerfully bored.
But I do know the sound of rattling bones
and reach for an ax, knives and stones.
I'm the kind of man who thinks he can.
Thinks he can make a kinder world.
Who can remember he's a survivor.
A poet, a prophet, a deep-sea diver
in the battle for the human soul.
Why should I sell out for money?
What about all this godforsaken memory?
Can I really make a better world?

Maybe I'd better give my pencil a rest
and sharpen the sickle's edge.

The time is near. The time is now.
Oh, the silence. Oh, the terror.

By the Danube

1
I sat on the edge of the river,
watching a melon rind float off.
I was so engrossed in myself,
in the silence of the dark,
I heard nothing above the water
except this great old Danube River
flowing straight from my heart.

Like muscles working a hammer,
chisel, a wood-chopping ax,
so did every movement of every wave
flex, tense, ripple and finally relax.
Like my mother who rocked me
while she told a story and quietly
washed the laundry of the town.

A half-hearted rain
couldn't make up its mind
before it stopped. I saw
through it as if from a cave,
watching it fall drop by drop.
Enough water to fill a sea
in its eternal monotony.

The Danube kept flowing. The waves
broke into foam like the laughter

of children on their mothers' lap.
Then a current made them shiver
and they froze. Froze like stones
in the graveyard of time.

2
I see a hundred thousand years
pass in the flicker of a moment
in the eyes of my ancestors.

And I see things they didn't,
busy with plowing, killing, loving.
And knit into the stuff
of living, they could sense
what would happen tomorrow.

We are kin like joy and sorrow.
I own the past, they the present.
We write poems together.
They hold my pen. I remember.
I feel their presence.

3
My mother was a Cuman,
my father half Székely,
half Rumanian or maybe all.
Food was sweet
from my mother's mouth,
truth meat

from my father's mouth.
When I moved, they touched,
and for a moment we were one.
Sad how fleeting this was.
They kept reminding me: Soon
we will be gone.

I remember.
They are part of me now,
my strength when I falter.
I remember. Every cell
of all my ancestors
abides in myself. I am that
ancient seed about to become
my mother and father.
They divide and I happily
become *the one*.

I am the world, all that is and was:
the strife of all the warring tribes,
the triumph of conquerors in death,
the death throes of the defeated. I am
Árpád and Zalán, Werb?czi and Dózsa.
Tartars, Turks, Slovaks, Rumanians
mix in my veins.
I am a new breed of Hungarian.

I'm anxious to work. It's a struggle
just to make a clean breast of the past.
This Danube is eternity's river.
Remember.

It absolves war after war.
It builds a new order,
it builds bridges instead of borders,
bolt by bolt, girder by girder.

Welcoming Thomas Mann

As a child who's sorry
he's being put to bed,
and pleads for another story
(to ward off the dead of night),
the heart longs for your light.
He doesn't know what to say:
(A story from you or for you to stay.)
So, stay! And before you go
tell us all you know.
Even if we heard it before,
tell it again, tell it more.
Tell us now more than ever
how we must stick together,
be worthy of each other.
You know the poet never lies,
he's either truthful or he dies.
Tell us what can ignite our art
in this great, gloomy dark.
Let us light one another tonight
like Castor lit Madame Chauchat.
No noise can drown you out.
Tell us about reality. About beauty.
Tell us about longing. About agony.
We just buried poor Kosztolányi.
He was devoured by cancer
as a dictator devours humanity.
So much terror without reason
lurking on a dark horizon.
How will they unleash their poison?

How long will they let you speak?
We are with you. We are not weak.
We are men and will remain men.
And women, women—free women.
And what is more we are all one.
So, sit down please, Thomas Mann.
Begin your story, and we will listen,
happy to see a true European.

Woodcutter

I split the wood into cool piles,
wood-knots whiten with a hiss,
sawdust falls on my hair and tickles
the little hairs on my neck.
    The minutes run on velvet.

There's an edge
to ice, like to an ax.
Earth, sky, brow, eyes,
light-chips swirl in the dark.

And dawn has an edge.
A stranger comes into the forest,
a thieving capitalist.
He says he felled the tree,
the stock is his.

The hell it is! We'll crash his stock.
Without a whimper, without a splinter,
we'll strike at the heart of destiny,
we'll strike at the heart of infamy,
we'll strike in unison,
our ax will shine in the sun.

On the City's Edge

On the city's edge where I live,
dusk floats on bat-like wings,
the soot stiffening
into thick guano.

This is how
we're smothered by this age,
hardened by pain. Though
storms lash at these
corrugated roofs of tin,
they are still dark.

Anguish.

If only we could bleed,
but we are what we are.
A new breed in a new soil.
We have our own dialect,
instead of parting our hair,
we slick it back.
Our God is not the intellect,
our Trinity is coal, steel,
and oil. Crude, holy oil.

We are your elements
poured hotly into the mold
of a savage world
that does not understand.
And it is here

we will make our stand.

We saw
the demise of priests, armies,
the ruling class. Now we are
inheritors of the law.
And every being, every artifact
sings to us, pleading
like a gypsy's violin.

We are indestructible,
though under this sun
we've lost more
than the lying past lets on,
undone by famine, cholera,
religion, and the gun.

Victors never so arrogant
under these stars. Vanquished
never so humiliated,
eyes cast down on the earth,
for the earth to give up its dead.

Terror in the eyes of animals
where machines run wild!
Fragile cities crushed
like lattices of ice. Crumbling
plaster, thundering skies.

Who can tame all this, if not us?
The lord of the land?

The shepherd's snarling dog?

We grew up with these machines.
They are animals, only with hands.
We know them by name.

Soon, you'll fall on your knees,
praying only to what you own,
but the machine only sees
those that feed it coal and oil.

Here we are, for better
or worse. Children of the soil.
Lift up our hearts!
We lift them up to the Horde!
We are the sons and daughters of oil.

Up with one heart!
Let it beat over tall chimneys,
this great smoky heart of ours.
Let it bellow in the deepest hollows
of the earth.

Up! Up!
High above this divided world.
Beat against the ribs, borders,
shatter fences, blow wind, blow!

Let this great heart glow!

In this foundry we'll found

a new and working order,
push ourselves to the limit,
catch the tail of the infinite,
where intellect is instinct
and creation everything.

This song rings out
at the city's edge.
The poet, its kin,
watches the soot
settle on his skin,
like thick guano.

The words hammer
in the poet's throat:
engineer, prophet,
smithy, whose rage
for harmony
creates his age.

Fire!

Fire!
The mill's on fire!
Don't hurt me, it's not my fault.
Oh God, maybe the fire's in me!
Don't hurt me, it's not my fault,
I really thought I saw a fire,
maybe it was a dream, an omen.

That's why I scream: Fire! Fire!

It's a great, roaring, raging fire.
Its gangly arms flail toward the sky,
there's this white glow inside
but it singes everything in sight.

Doesn't anyone feel it? Only me?
Did the Hungarians die already?
All the men and all the women?
But here they are walking around.
Are they flesh and blood? Or robots?
They go to movies, eat and drink.
They don't give a dog's dick what I think.

Can they even hear me? Or is it just me?
We have plenty of wheat, plenty of flour.
Will it be better once the angels come
and bake us sweet-bread from smoke?

Look! Fire!

You are walking into fire.
If you see me, it's the vision of a lunatic.
He's seen your death. You'd better believe it.
At night, in front of your eyes he'll appear,
whisper the hot roar of silence in your ear.
Flames will spew from his raging mouth.

Your death?
Now *that* I don't know much about.
I just plant myself in your ear,
trembling, roaring like a town crier:

Fire! Fire! Fire!

Ode

1
I sit here
on a shimmering cliff.
Early summer's
breeze floats by
like a warm supper.

My heart is quiet.
It isn't so bad—
the rush of memories,
then the head
hangs down, then the arms.

The mane of the mountains,
your face, flutter before me
like a quicksilver of leaves.
Not a soul on the road.
The wind lifts your skirt
and wisps of your hair
dance on your breast.
It swells like the river.
And your laughter
reminds me how water
washes over white pebbles.

2
How I love you,
who put into words
the deepest mysteries,

the burning longing
of the human heart.

The art of solitude.

You leave me in silence
as after a roaring waterfall.
You trail off in the distance,
deaf to a lunatic's rant.
From the peaks and valleys
of my little life, I swear
with all my being
that I love you,
you sweet,
cruel thing.

3
I love you,
like a child his mother,
like a well the deep.
I love you
like a room loves light,
like a soul its flame,
like the body peace.
I love you
like the dying love life.

I cling
to your every smile, your every move,
your every word, as the earth
clings to all things that fall

from the sky.
Like acid eats metal,
my instincts burn you
and all that you are
into my brain.

The minutes, the years drone on,
you are silence itself in my ears.
Stars may rise and fall
still you glow fiercely in my eyes.
Your taste lingers in my mouth
like coolness of the deepest cave.
The fingerprints you left on my glass
shimmer in the light
their fine network of veins.

4
What am I made of?
A glance from you
can make or break me.
You appear in the empty air
as the light of your soul.
I bend
with every hill and valley
of your fertile body.

As the mystery of the words unfold,
you unfold. And I descend.

Your blood vessels tremble
like rose bushes.

They carry the eternal current
so that love can bloom
on your face. Blessed is
the fruit of your womb.

Filaments root and thread,
knot and untie
in the lining of your stomach
where cells pool into life's holy bread—

The lofty branches of your lungs
hum your glory with each breath.

The eternal matter courses happily
through the tunnels of your bowels,
waste garnering new life in the warm
springs of your kidneys.

Mountains rise and fall in you,
stars tremble, rivers flow,
veritable factories
work in your tissues,
a million living things
teem with life,
insects,
seaweed,
mercy, cruelty.
The bright sun, the pall
of northern nights,
immortality,
you contain them all.

5
My words rain on you.
They are drops of my blood.
My being may stutter
but the die is cast.
My diligent organs
regenerate daily
with the knowledge
that they will die.

But until then
they rage—
out of two thousand million,
you are the one, the cradle,
the bed, the grave,
all that will take me in.

(This is one epic dawn!
Entire armies glitter
in its metallic veins.
It is overly bright here.
I think I am lost.
The sound of thunder,
my heart.)

6
(Epilogue)

(I'm on the train following you.
I may even catch up with you,

but then the fire may die,
or you might say:
"I'm drawing a bath for you!
Here's my shawl for a towel!
Your supper is on the stove,
your bed is where I lie.)

Hang On!

In China hangs a mandarin,
another dead by heroin.
The straw hisses, go to bed.
Another dead by heroin.

Into the department store
stare the poor, stare the poor.
The straw hisses, go to bed.
Cash registers for the dead.

Buy the meat. Buy the bread.
Keep your belly fed.
The straw hisses, go to bed.
Keep your belly fed.

A girl cooks, a girl kisses.
Soon she will be wed.
The straw hisses, go to bed.
Soon she will be wed.

Air!

Just try to shut me up! I'll tell you what ruffles
my feathers but not now.
Another time. Maybe on the way home.
A huge darkness descends on the grass
like velvet,
dry leaves rustle under the feet
of abused orphans.

Bushes squat
on the edge of town,
out of the way even for the wind.
    The sand stares dumbly at the street lamp,
a quacking duck rushes the water.

It's so out of the way here, I half expect
    to be jumped.
Suddenly this man bumps my shoulder,
but then moves on.
I look after him. He could've robbed me.
I just don't have it in me to fight.
I just don't.

They keep track of my phone calls,
who I call and when and why.
They keep a transcript of my dreams
    and what they mean
    and according to whom.
I don't know what's in my file of late
but soon they'll make a move

and violate my rights.
In scattered villages,
    like my mother's,
    justice has been swept aside
    like so many dead leaves.
Villages dogged by the rust of the ages.
They whine like the wind
    that blows away their dust.

My sense of justice is a bit
    different than this.
I refuse to believe the corrupt
    always get their way.
Are the just so intimidated,
    they cast their eyes down instead
    of casting their ballots? Idiots!
They feel more at home at funerals.

This is not my sense of justice.
    As a child I was also beaten
and for no reason.
I would've jumped at a kind word.
But my mother was far, I was an orphan,
    and these were not kind men.

I'm grown up now. With enough dead metal
bonding my teeth,
and enough death to harden my heart.
I know my rights. I'm not a dead tree.
To hell with my precious hide.
    I won't stand by without saying my mind.

I intend to be free!
To listen to a voice inside!
　　　We are not beasts. We have minds!
We are not deaf, we are not dumb.
We long for a full life, not a full file.

We will be free! And we'll have our say!
We'll teach the young freedom,
let them play, let them play.

Let the children play.

The Dog

Such a wet, shaggy dog,
with its coat of yellowing flame.
Scruffy now, ribbed and lame
with hunger and longing.
The cool night wind
crawls into its fur.
It runs, it begs.
Sighing church candles
flicker in its eyes.
It sniffs for alms,
any crumb it can find.
Suddenly what springs
from my chest is its great,
tattered heart. Now we howl
together in the dark.

We lie down finally.
Put down by the night
and misery. But
before we close our eyes,
we lie there like the hulking
city, numb and weary
and loyal unto death.
Then something
creeps forward at the break
of day. A wet, scruffy thing
springs of our being,
sniffing for God's daily bread,
for alms, for crumbs, for anything.

Night in the Ghetto

The light slowly lifts
its net from the yard,
the kitchen fills with mist,
flotsam on a still pond.

Silence—the scrub brush
rises to its feet and crawls.
Above it a piece of wall
ponders whether to drop.

The night sighs
in oily rags,
sits on the city's edge,
then limps across the square
to ignite a feeble moon.

Mills loom
like ruins
to conceive
a denser dark,
the pedestal of silence.

Through the windows
the moon floats
in sheaves,
threads each chair
with light
until morning.
As the work stands still

the power loom spins
the weaver's crumbling dreams.

Steel yards,
cement yards, tool and die,
like graveyards. Mausoleums
guard the secret of resurrection.
A cat scratches the fence,
the night watchman sees a ghost—
dynamos spark
like fireflies.

Trains whistle.

Dampness gropes in the twilight
and curdles the dust
among the leaves.

A policeman.
Someone with leaflets
crosses the street
on cat paws, sniffs
the pavement like a dog
and avoids the street lamp.

The tavern's window vomits
sour light into pools.
The choking light flickers,
only a hired hand keeps vigil.
The bartender snores, hisses,
bares his teeth at the wall,

then runs up syphilitic steps
and cries. Cries for revolution.

Taut waters lash
into cooled steel.
The wind howls, laps
it with a stray dog's tongue.

Sacks of hay like barges
float silently on the edge of night—

the warehouse is a bottomless ship,
the foundry's ore boat conceives,
red seeds ignite into form.

Everything is damp. Everything heavy.
Mildew traces squalid maps
on bare fields
where the grass is in rags.
A piece of paper
stirs but is powerless to move…

Damp, clinging wind.
The flapping of dirty sheets,
oh night!
You hang like frayed calico,
on the line like sorrow.
Poor man's night! Coal,
smolder my heart,
melt steel
for an anvil that can't break.

A hammer that pounds blades
for victory, oh night!

The night is dead, the night is heavy.
It is now ready for dreams
to worm their way into the body.

I AM NOT THE ONE SHOUTING

IT'S THE EARTH RUMBLING!
LOOK OUT! LOOK OUT!
SATAN'S GONE CRAZY.
SINK TO THE BOTTOM OF CLEAR CREEKS,
CLING TO CRYSTAL.
HIDE BENEATH THE DIAMOND LIGHT
AMONG INSECTS AND STONES.
BURROW INTO FRESH BREAD,
YOU POOR DEAD, YOU POOR DEAD.
SEEP INTO THE EARTH WITH SHOWERS.
IT'S USELESS TO BATHE IN YOURSELF.
WASH YOUR FACE IN OTHER FACES.
YOU ARE A CELL ON A BLADE OF GRASS
BUT GREATER THAN THE EARTH'S AXIS.

OH, MACHINES! BIRDS! BLOSSOMS! STARS!
A BARREN MOTHER TREMBLES FOR BIRTH.
MY FRIEND, MY DEAR LOVING FRIEND,
NO MATTER HOW TERRIBLE THE END,
I AM NOT THE ONE SHOUTING,
IT'S THE EARTH RUMBLING. THE EARTH!

The Eagle

swoops down cliffs.
Lightning with wings,
conceived out of nothing.
Much more than mere living.

Its brilliant blue beak
swallows everything;
steel claws tear
warm meat

and the crying.
Bloody down glistens,
eyes paint
the dawn red.

What eagle! What thought!
What shadow it carves,
the night, delight, love
into the sparking stars.

One wing
is my song, the other, my Flora,
charging and recharging
my night with lightning.

The Last Warrior

On a hot summer night
smoke and oil braided
with the smell of the soil,
and a great spirit darted
into my soul: I'm the son
of earth and oil.

My arms reach across continents.
My heart is a giant red flower
fanned by billowing electric power
to stink up every corner of the world.

Nothing can shut me up.
No prison, no draft, no religion.
My words tumble down
from the mountaintop.
My words are my gospel,
everything else is drivel.

When I cry, the earth bleeds,
when I curse, thrones tremble.
God's happiest when I'm laughing,
it is my winter that rushes into spring.

I believe in destiny.
I don't have a miraculous heart
but my heart expects miracles.
Hot ash pours from my mouth,
I demolish barracks, prisons, cubicles,

so the future can burn inside of us,
the last of the working warriors.

Our banner unfurls to lead the way,
where we go, others will follow.

We are veterans of lost wars
heaving our burning hard hats
at the sky. We are comets
going home to birth new stars.
Mirrors of all great spirits,
sons of the earth and oil.

TWO
Sons and Lovers

Mamma

For a week, stopping now and then,
I think only of mamma.
Carrying a creaking laundry basket,
she briskly went up to the attic.

And I was such a bold little man,
I screamed and raved and stamped my feet.
Leave those damp clothes to someone else,
take me up to the attic.

She went on and hung the clothes mutely,
she didn't scold, she didn't look at me,
and the clothes glistened, whispering,
dangling high in the wind.

I wouldn't whimper, but it's too late,
I see now how enormous she is,
her gray hair flows into heaven,
she blues the waters of the sky.

Too Late for a Eulogy

I burn with a fever of 98.6
and, mother, you won't even nurse me.
Like a whore you lie
beside the angel of death.
I try to piece you together
from autumn scenes and so many women
but there's not enough time.
    The fire bores through me.

The last time I went home
    it was the end of the war
and a starving Budapest was in ruins.
I lay flat on a boxcar
bringing you potatoes, chicken, bread—
but you weren't there!
How could you be dead?!

You took your breasts
and gave them to the worms!
Your sweet words were all lies.
You warmed our soup, blew on it,
stirred it and said: eat all of it.
Now your lips taste only
the dampness.
    You lied to me on purpose!

I should've eaten you!
Why give me your own supper?
Did I ask for it? Why wreck your back

washing my damn socks?
So you could straighten it
in a wooden box?
Why don't you just
beat me once more,
so I can strike you back!
You're terrible. You strive not to be,
    You ruin everything!
You stalk me like a shadow!

You're more of a cheat
than all the whores I know!
You gave up on love and the lives
you so painfully bore.
And the life you abhor!
You're a gypsy! Whatever love
you gave me, you stole back
in your last hour!
Damn you, mother! Can you hear?
Say something! Yell at me!

It's over. The head slowly clears.
A child hanging on for mother's
love finds out how foolish he is.
We all end up like this, cheated
in the end. We rant, we forgive.
Forget that to live
always ends in a dead-end.

My Mother Just Died

My mother just died,
and I don't know how to act.
She could patch my coat, I guess.
Or she could watch me undress.
See how lovely I am naked.
Nobody has seen me naked!
The peasants have harvested.
They sit on stools waiting for death—
Busybody roaches nibble at dreams,
plates are only good to hang on walls.
A little butter on my bread, please!
Actually I could use a real meal,
just to get my strength back.
God, I don't know how to act!
I guess I could use another
pair of boots by my bed.
God knows we all could.
If only there were more of us—
I see the bridge in the fog. And the bayonets
on the other shore. There are more and more.

Here are the tailor's scissors
and the bolts of cloth.
What are we waiting for?

Strength Song

Muscles ripple my seventeen year-old back.
My eyes are keen at the horizon's edge.
I toss spring over my shoulder
and feed it to my heart.
I bear the yoke of my defiant age.
I groan but my knees refuse to bend.
I hoard the flaming dragon of my rages,
the tongue that wrings the page's sorrow.
Pyramid worlds crumble under my feet,
I stagger the heavens. The sun crowns my head.
Worlds of pain drain from my clenched fist.
Nothing, but nothing brings me to my knees
but my mother's grave overgrown with weeds.

Autumn

Autumn fog scrapes
bald interlacing branches,
frost squints on the railing.

Weariness squats on a boxcar,
dreaming of the engine
as it winds home on the tracks.

A few dispirited yellow hills
disrobe and whine in the wind.
Damp leaves stick to the stone.

Blushing summer
packed away her rags and left
as unexpectedly as she came.

Autumn is already lurking
about the yard, drooling
between the bricks.

I knew she'd be here.
There's barely time
to heat the room.
I can't believe she's here so soon,
looking into my eyes,
whispering into my ear.

Without Knocking

If I fall in love with you,
you can always come in
without knocking.
But you better think twice.
My king bed is a straw sack
with a bad habit of sighing
with dust. Sometimes it hisses.

I'll bring you fresh water in a jug,
and wipe the dust from your shoes
before you go. Nobody will bother us.
You can darn my socks in peace.

Silence is golden here,
but I can speak non-stop,
if you please.
I'll sit you down on my only chair
if you're tired. If it's too warm,
you can take off your clothes.
If you're hungry, I can give you
a clean newspaper for a plate.
When there really is something,
you better leave me some.
I seem to be hungry all the time.

If I fall in love with you, come in
without knocking,
but you better think twice.
If you stop coming, I'll be cold as ice.

Biblical

Your hair oozes down your back
like sweet-smelling tar
poured from a steaming drum.
Your hair flutters like three flocks
of thick-bodied ravens—
and your breast like a basket
filled to the brim with bread.

You are kin
to warm cows
that lie next to each other
on grassy fields
in great milk-smelling herds.
Let's bathe ourselves, heart to heart,
in the river. We are also clean.
We float away in clear water.

I am clean
because I love you.
I see God giving you His heart
so He can come to me inside you.
He is my eternal love, my death.

Our desire rips off the clothes
we just bought. It doesn't matter
it's raining stones on my head,
and you're floating on a cloud
on a lazy evening. Who knows?
Times like these

have tossed the likes of us
all over Europe.

Odd, but you will fall in love
with someone who desires you
as much as I desire you now.
And your hair will float off on a river—
but remember, always remember,
my great and beautiful God.

Rising at Dawn Like the Bakers

My love has a slender but firm waist.
From high in the air she may look small,
but to me she is all that I have.

Look how she washes the clothes,
suds tremble and dream along her arms;
she kneels as if she were praying,
scrubbing the floor;
and when she laughs,
she laughs with all her being.

The peal of her laughter
is like biting into a fresh apple.

She rises at dawn like the bakers.
She kneads dough by their ovens,
and keeps vigil with long paddles.
They beat the flour into a cloud
that settles on her breasts
and sleeps there snug and happy.

A lover's sweet-smelling bed.

After the wash and the dishes,
she makes me feel sweet and clean
by the way she lets me love her.

My wife will be like this.
She will be like my mother.

And I will marry her,
like my father.

Kiszombor Song

You are a source of agony.
Kinder to my best friend
than you are to me.
I just wanted to touch your hair.
To be a hair's breath away.
Strange visions torment me.
You are a drop of water,
the only light in my dreams.
I am tilling a field of sorrow,
when locks of your hair
blow into the furrow.
Sándor has warm gloves.
He doesn't need your warm hands.
I do.
Everybody's drinking.
We're on holiday.
I can't say I'm happy for you.

For Mancika

with apologies to Margaréta

I crouch under the plum tree
and listen to the birds' mating call,
maybe love will fall into my lap.
Cuckoo. The orchard fog treads
on my heart in cotton slippers.

I'm roosting like old mosquitoes,
cane nestles among the rushes,
the wind blows cold at my feet.
Leaves rustle, the earth's sigh
is a bit too sentimental.

My fists press against my head.
Like bricks, the hardness of these fists.
This girl Margaréta has wrecked
a life already wrecked.
I'm so broke I owe the dead.
And my work is plain and melancholy.

No plum for this poem.

The hoe's brown handle
accuses me from the shed.
A bush makes a desperate leap after gossamer,
its dry leaves a faint murmur in the wind.

You're Such a Fool

You run
like the morning wind.
If you're not careful,
you'll get run over.
I scrubbed my little table
for us,
and now
the soft light on my bread
looks cleaner.
Come back.
If you want, I'll buy a cover
for my metal bed.
A simple, gray comforter
to go with my poverty.
The Lord loves it and He
loves me. He won't let
His radiance blind me,
so I could see you clearly.
Because I need to see
the candles in your eyes.
And I will kiss you gently
without tearing at your coat,
and I saved these silly jokes
just to cheer you up.
First, you'll blush,
then look at the floor,
and we'll double over laughing.
We'll laugh so loud
our neighbors will hear us.

And we'll hear them laughing
in their sleep. Imagine
their weathered faces
convulsing with laughter.
Requiem for a dream.

Judit

Autumn is undressing the trees,
it's cold, time to heat the room.
You haul down the stove on your own.
    Like old times,

when it was cold, before we learned
    to keep each other warm, before
we quarreled, before I felt you were
no longer mine.

The nights are longer now and quieter,
the world is larger, and a lot scarier.
You will not be sewing our comforter,
which tore over and over.

Cold stars glow between the branches.
Are you still awake? Where you are?
Go to bed. I also sleep alone.
Curl under the covers
and let it be. Go to sleep now.
Dream of me.

Spring Mud

A cloud bursts on the street,
the square and the field.
The canal roars, a ditch overflows.
Plaster peels from old houses.
The rain is pure, holy liquid
trickling down the legs of horses.
Water and mud on the rooftops.
Holy water and mud.

The whole earth is soft, warm mud.
The heavens, horses, the houses
are all soft, warm mud.
Children stand in the windows
watching the rain, listening to it drop.
Their hearts, too, are soft, warm mud.

The peace of seeds has moved
into the hearts of houses, horses.
Into the hearts of men. To descend
where we are all lovers in the end.
We are all soft, warm mud
in this bond of dust and holy rain.

Let it rain forever like this.
Drop by drop. Kiss after kiss.

Insects

We creep forward
as marvelous insects.
Were we clouds we would come
only in drought,
avoid picnickers
gathering litter lest
it rain tomorrow.
Our threadbare bodies
heat up in summer.
Insects play a week in a day.
From a hidden bush
birds watch their mating.

A pebble is innocent,
unearthed in the scented
footprints of these girls.
It cannot be me or the grass,
though I am friend to everything:
the hazelnut gratefully splits
in my hand. A branch brushes
a straw left tangled in my hair.
Meadow after meadow is like the arms
of a woman who leads young men
with the spread of her skirt.
They fan her fragrance
and blossom with bald,
iridescent shields
turned toward the sun.

Sleep Silently

It is a lovely night. Sleep silently.
The neighbors are in bed.
And the workmen are leaving.
Sounds of the hammer
on stone
trail off in the distance.
All is quiet
since I last saw you.

Your tired arms are cool
like this deep, silent river.
It doesn't murmur, it just flows,
so slowly, the trees fall asleep,
then the fish,
and the stars.
And there's no one left
but me.

I am tired.
I work hard to live.
But I will fall asleep.
Sleep silently.
If I'm unhappy
you must be. Or should be.

It is too quiet to live.
Even the flowers forgive.

Night

The lamp flickers its last breath:
enter a nun's daughter impersonating death,
and now a dark princess slips into my bed.

Her icy eyes put out the light in mine,
she smoothes every wrinkle on my temple,
her dark abyss does not seem so terrible.

She doesn't ask about strange longings,
ignores my humble, frayed belongings,
her arms are still around me mornings.

She holds me spellbound in reverie,
and while she kisses away all misery,
she fulfills my childhood fantasy.

Her raven hair floods my room
she soothes my thoughts of doom,
she's the one who lights the moon.

I'd open an artery,
if she'd ask me nicely: "Son,
I've been waiting for you nightly."

I wait in vain, she has no mouth
to warn about her secret boat,

and I end up dangling from a rope.

It's only me mumbling in my bed
or the rain falling or the sky rumbling:
"You are dead. You are dead."

You Made Me a Child

Thirty pain-wracked winters
tried hard to make me into a man,
still I can't walk, sit or stand alone.
My legs keep sleepwalking toward you.

I hold you in my mouth
like the dog its litter,
and run from the dog-catcher.

Give me something,
throw me a bone, mother!
I'm hungry. I'm cold. Cover me up.
I'm going to be bad. Beat me!
It's cold in here,
I shiver in your absence.
I'm cold to the bone.
Tell them to leave me alone.

One look from you
and I forget everything.
You listen, I stop speaking.

Make me less dependent.
Let me live, let me die alone.

My mother kicked me out
and I lay outside her door.
I wanted to crawl
into myself. Beneath me

stone, above me empty air.

If only I could sleep.
I pound on the door...

There are many cold men.
I'm one of them. Yet they can cry.
That's why I love those men.
They know me as one of them.

The Secrets of the Heart

    on Freud's 80th birthday

The secrets of the heart
should be seen by the eyes;
what your eyes witness
your heart must feel.

It is said,
those who love
turn up dead,

that happiness
is a slice of bread,

and the rest yearn
for their mother's breast.
They love and murder
in the marriage bed.

Be that 80-year old,
the one
who's persecuted,
and as he's rising,
he's siring a million sons.

That thorn has been long
removed from your side.
And now death itself
is pried from your heart.

What your eyes witness
your hands will touch.

The secrets of the heart
you can kill or kiss.

My Love

Flower petals touch in the night.
I do not want a kiss,
only to feel your nearness
like a child his mother's.
If a pear tree and its
grafted slip grow together,
I'd also be better to slip
engrafted in you. Give me
your lips.
The night and I are lovelier
stamped with your infinite stars.

How warm you are. A spring breeze
with its promise of rain
and luscious mud lures
children to play hide and seek.

How long I waited for you to find me
in the scented forest of my chest.
Animal hungers, fire and ice,
gore one another with antlers,
but how gently they graze now
among your lilies.

You are finally here. Drawn to me.
Still too dark to see our breath,
except for the ferns that frost up
our window. It is dawn. Dawn!
And I'm still talking kisses!

Sacrilege

A crazed, drunken youth
full of demons and liquor
is on the loose by the altar.
He stumbles to the Virgin
and, amid whoops and vile
gestures, tries to grab her.

Even the Child trembles
in her arms.
He wipes a bloodshot eye
with his sleeve—

This is how I feel
when you leave me.
I mumble and stumble,
my arms flail toward you,

Thou inaccessible.

Please don't leap to judgement.
I am a victim of my own demons.
They pursue me daily,
they pursue me unto death,
enraged by my own sacrilege.

I am a man of blasphemy,
my destiny is to be stoned.
In my crude way I plead
for your virgin mercy.

I Wait For You

I wait for you.
There's dew on the rough grass.
Sprawling branches wait for you
with open arms.

I am cold. The leaves are wet
and shiver at night.

Should you come, they would quiet.
And there would be great silence.
We'd listen only to our hearts,
feel only the sweetness of our lips.
Nothing else would matter.

Our skins would burn
red and infinite
and our souls melt
into the dawn's scented altar.

THREE
Son of Man

The Lord is High

The Lord is high,
the lard is low,
the rich get sick,
the poor get sicker.

Who comes here
on the twists and turns
of winding trails?
Milking girls
with foamy pails?

Is it the poor?
Are they coming to praise the Lord?
But the Lord is hard and old.
He belongs to the cardinals.

Sausage for the poor?
Skirt for the wife?
Homage to the Lord?

If only He'd look out
on all the beaten roads,
He'd see the poor heading
toward the warm south.

If He's not for them now,
He can forget them.
At the hour of their death
they will be dead men.

Young Lobster, Red Lobster

Shadows of silverfish sweep by the corals,
usher in the blackness, flutter on soft sand.
They touch tired snails and fall fast asleep.

I watch the man-of-war's transparent light,
cut a path with ragged scissors, and send
ripples chiming upward in clean water.

Where the shimmer is most brilliant,
come there.

What I offer is a faint ray
in the light, but it's mine.
Think of me and keep vigil
in your garden where shells blossom
with open wings.

Strong currents harden my armor.
Only you can understand its redness—
blue coral billows on my back,

I wait for you by the whitest stone.

Waves! Rush quickly from the hill!
Let the lobster send fat morsels
toward the coral's fluttering petals.

Dance of Flames

We slumber in dry lumber, blaze in coal piles,
    in the hands of women in love.
We crackle under the kettle,
our sparks hiss, sputter.
We sear great slabs of meat above us.
We make even the stone blush.

In the fields, in the pasture
we reach into the clouds,
    blood runs down our supple, lanky arms,
down our every limb, dark and rich
like the brown soil in whose womb
all this good fat
fries and melts,
sizzling, dripping,
mingling with the earth.

We stretch in the veins
of lovely young men, sow seeds in their sinews
    to become strong, willowy branches
that will rustle for centuries
in trackless forests.
    Hot liquid gushes from their skin,
sending beatific golden birds toward heaven.

And they love us, when we gather
    in a great forest fire that reaches the sky.
Girls and boys run wild in the open field,
a glow fluttering in their lovely hearts.

Hand in hand,
around and around they dance,
their laughing face on fire,
and they grow old with grace,
and when they're old,
their shriveled little bodies
mingle with our ashes with a kiss.

Moonlight

Moonlight opens graves to dreams.
In a kitchen a frightened little boy
devours the bread left on the floor.

Only the wind-chime knows.

Everybody's asleep in the house.
Knees tremble. Eyes grow wide.
He rummages through vats of lard,
sniffs and scurries like a mouse.

If the cupboard creaks, a hand
flies to his lips. His. The mouth
yelps and pleads for pity.
Silence is deafening in the city.

A sudden noise.
It reaches beyond the kitchen.
It grows until it cracks the world.
Deathly-white, he drops the knife
and sneaks back to his bed...

I wake up to a burning sun,
the hiss of cracking ice,
a fist shattering glass,
a boot through a window-front:
Tropical fruit for everyone!

The God of Frost is caving in,

heaven is helpless,
and the devil's bored with sin.
He drills a well down to hell,
spewing fire from his lair,

burning bushes green in spring.

Unloading Lumber

Autumn wind creeps
between the boxcars,
logs hit the platform
with a loud thud.

One rolls off. It's over.
Be still. I'm afraid I'll fall
with the stolen lumber
under my arm.
I'm a child after all.

The boy in me is still alive.
He skins the adult in me alive.
He doesn't cry, he whistles
in the wind out of fear,
he holds his hat, his head is bare.

Were you those fearless men
who could juggle logs in air?

Like stolen lumber, I take you then,
I take you for this poem.

Welcome to my homeless den.

Bethlehem

Soft crows perch on cotton clouds,
twilight leaks between the branches.
Two staff-bearing shepherds and three kings
stand stiffly on the dirt floor.
A woman descends the ladder.
"Angels from on high," five elders sing.
Outside the window an old man
pitches manure to clucking chickens.
Muddy potatoes cower in the hay.
The thatch roof bristles,
steaming soup ascends
like incense above the baby Jesus,
joyous in his playpen of yellow down
and paper sheep. By fire light,
meek men of good will
and even better means
dance around the manger.

God's lordly wind
kicks out the commoner,
two shepherds gorge on gingerbread,
three kings guzzle their liquor.

Spring Suddenly From the Tide

Terrify me, God.
I'm in need of your anger.
Spring suddenly from the tide.
Nothingness washes me under.

I'm thrown from my horse,
I'm up to my eyes in the sand.
I play with the knives of agonies
not meant for the heart of man.

I'm flammable. I burn like the sun.
Damn it, why not just take me!
Yell at me! Tell me I'm a failure.
Smack my hand with your thunder!

Beat on my heart or let me in Yours:
Being too good is a mortal sin!
It melts faster than ice in hell
to pretend all's well in paradise.

Down to the bone in a foaming sea,
I let myself drown. I am ready
for anything except this damned nothing.

I hold my breath to die.
And if you don't beat me,
I'll swear up and down
that you have no face.
And then I'll stare you down.

I'm Serious

My buoyant mood has become serious.
I've been going to my gray haired Lord.
Even there all I did was make demands.
What did I want? What did I ever want?

A hammering, ship-loading spirit?
A warm woman to weave nets for me?
To write poems, to try and understand
this angry-green unfathomable sea?

But what was I? A foolhardy prophet?
One great word-tormented desire,
envious of another's words,
a wish for a laurel wreath
a wreath of thorns?

Anguish
is God's strongest one-word sentence.
How many hearts bleed for it,
the sweat on wretched faces,
oil trickling down the arms
of overworked machines?

I don't bother to ask for grace,
but I am bending my knees.
There's no woman alive
I have not desired.
What should I do now?
Disfigure my face?

Maybe it's time
to buckle down and pray,
become a little town at dawn,
where tranquilized cows
are led toward the Lord's
knee-deep pastures.

Attila József

He was cheerful, maybe a little stubborn,
when they hurt him he found solace in truth.
He liked to eat, and in this and that
he resembled God.
He received a coat from a Jewish doctor,
but his relatives told him not to bother.
He sought asylum in Greek orthodoxy
but found only priests.
He was universal in his desolation,

but don't let him bring you down
with the congregation.

About a Poet

You they love. You they understand.
Because you never bowed to fear.
And here I am
deluding myself with grandeur.

I'm heavy now and sink in the sand.

Look, I was twelve pounds at birth,
still she survived. So I have to wait
for someone else to bear my weight,
to be free of the suck of the earth.

Luck? Somehow I don't think so.
A prize will appear out of nowhere
or you'll crack somewhere like ice
and beg on your knees for life.

I did succeed (which I regret,
since that alone is a heinous deed)
and now I qualify for dry bread
I eat as the body of Christ.

Sometimes Islands

Sometimes islands pop into our heads,
and birds fly over them sowing
the seeds of fabulous plants.
Sweat rolls from the machine's brow,
tears from a mother's eyes,
oil from the work of our hands.
And somehow the world keeps turning.
Yesterday I thought I was a pear tree,
and today children still run to me,
they hug and shake my fruit-laden boughs.

I bottled my first love in booze and when I
look at her I see an odd little beastie.
Hello, hello, and how are you? Thank you,
    I'm fine, and you? We talk
    as if we had no feelings.
Yet here we are, shivering atop Mont Blanc,
    praying: Lord, Lord,
why didn't you make mountains!

I give myself to you like a mother
her breasts to her hungry urchins.
The bushes are already sleeping,
I will also lie down inside you,
so that my favorite, steel-faced
tools are handy in the morning.

Now I See

Now I see why my father,
set out for America
on the far, choppy seas.

Hitting the road was nothing new.
That he did with ease. With
a bit of courage, a bit of luck.

But he did give up on us here.
Sank into a deep despair
making soap for a buck.

Now I see why my father
set out for America
on the deep, choppy seas.

He tired of the landlords' swindle,
packed what he had into a bundle
so he could go and make a bundle.

Had nothing here to call his own,
but all the way he thought of home
and vomited into the foam.

Now I see why my "daddy,"
as they say in America,
had to abandon his family.
And now that he makes money,
no one seems to care for daddy.

The fact is they curse him plenty.
No role model left in this house:
When things get rough, the tough get out.

Now I see why my father
set out for America
on the rough and wily seas.

I, myself, I'm setting out.
A new life for me and my Flora.
She is my America.

I try not to pry
when it's not my business,
usually I'm met with kindness.

So, my father set out
to see the great new world—

Well, we don't need anybody's pity.
We'll put our trust in God Almighty.

I'm made of different stock than he,
one that cheats and kills for love—
but at least with dignity.

Nesting in the Forest

The crows nest in the trees,
dark thoughts nest in my head.
The moon kisses
a hundred flowering buds,
your white face among them.
Everything is quiet:
the leaves, the sky, the forest.

My proud songs rest in silence.
What I thought was infinite
crashes with the break of day.
Crows now settle in the vineyard
to peck at our clotting hearts.
Green grapes fall from my hand.

Then the mad scramble for money.

The wait for night's honeyed moon.
What am I? God Almighty? Or a loon?

The Man Spoke

There was a man. He walked, stopped,
looked around and said: I'm a pear tree.
And the roots became the earth,
the trunk his girth, the leaves the sky.
They ate of pears, the insects,
the birds, the hunger-driven stars.

Then he walked on. And stopped,
looked around: I am coal and iron.
He tossed whole mountains
into roaring mills, furnaces
that spit out rumbling locomotives
to triumph over time and death.

The man spoke, stopped and left.
And never said: I am a man.

FOUR
Perched on Nothing's Branch

A Tree Here, a Tree There

A tree here, a tree there,
charred limbs, hit by lightning,
the coal-hearted, the bitter,
the proud.

A tree here, a tree there.

Why aren't they green?
ask the fields.
Even the bees stay clear
of their black dust.
The apple trees whisper:
Why can't they at least
bear crab apples,
the lazy bastards!

They're worthless as rafters,
they're no good as gallows.
How come they don't work?
Questions, curses, accusations.
Killing looks.

The trees let a patch of sky
drop between their burnt arms.
They stand upright
like pole-wells
but without water.
How can they live like this?
A tree here, a tree there,

arm-like branches
burnt beyond repair.
How can they
aspire toward heaven?

What the hell!
We'll meet our Maker,
as the good priest promised.
We won't march in like saints
but we will make a stand.
We'll demand that Providence
raise the dead: Make us green,
make us vivid. So we can dance.

With all My Heart

I have no father, I have no mother,
I have no God, I have no land,
I have no cradle or a cover,
no kiss, no lover's hand.

Three days I haven't eaten,
not too much and not too well,
all I have is twenty years,
twenty years of hell
I'd gladly sell.

If no one wants them,
then maybe the devil will.
I'd be thrilled to rob and steal
and kill and kill and kill.

They'll catch me and they'll hang me,
and cover me up with blessed earth,
and death-eating grass will start
growing from my lovely heart.

On My Birthday

I've just turned thirty-two,
time to pen a poem or two.
    A silly
    ditty.

A little coffeehouse surprise
for the wise
    by me
    for me.

Thirty-two years up the spout,
a farthing for a salary.
    Nice country,
    Hungary!

Could've been a teacher,
not a meager, pen*ny* pincher,
    hunger
    monger.

I was forced to depart
from the College of Arts
by an old fart,
    a mean
    dean.

He didn't think
my ditty "With All My Heart"
was very pretty.

A single poem cost me plenty.
   Smart
   heart.

He said my moral insanity
ruins the name of the academy.
   Name?
   Shame!

"As long as I'm professor here,
you won't be teaching anywhere,"
   he said.
   I'm dead.

If Professor Horger's ax
deprives me of proper syntax,
he is
   a shallow
   fellow.

My poems aspire a bit higher
than his higher education.
I will teach an entire nation,
and not in
   school,
   fool!

Sit, Stand, Kill, and Die

Kick the goddamn chair away,
squat before a rushing train,
climb a mountain in the rain,
toss my backpack down a gully,
feed my favorite spider honey,
make love to an old nanny,
make bean dishes really tasty,
walk barefooted when it's muddy,
on a train track put my beanie,
pace the lake melancholy,
get wet if clothes are dirty,
suffer sunburn of the body,
a blooming sunflower looking pretty,
making sure that sighs are heavy,
chase away that fly already,
wipe off any book that's dusty,
spit at mirrors when I'm ugly,
make peace with thy enemy,
slash them with a blade suddenly,
watch the blood drain very slowly,
watch a little girl turn lovely,
sit in a park for a century,
set fire to all of Hungary,
give my last crumb to a canary,
toss stale bread into the gully,
with my girl become a bully,
screw her sister in the pantry,
and if the world doesn't like me,
I'll leave it when I'm good and ready—

A lot of agony, a bit of glory
forcing my hand at poetry,
crying, laughing, acting silly,
accepting death, living fully
in the spirit of the body.

You Come With a Stick

Instead of a flower you carry a stick,
pick a fight on the River Styx,
promise your mother a pot of gold.
Then sit. Do nothing worth a lick.

Hide like a mushroom under a tree
(always groveling for mercy).
Lock yourself in the Seven Towers
and never launch out to sea.

Sink your baby teeth into stone.
Run in place to stay alone.
Daydream biting into bone.
There's nothing to be done!

You made yourself naked,
abused yourself by picking scabs.
You've only been famous
a few weeks. It won't last.

Can't you see it? Idiot!

Did you love? Were you touched?
Where were you touched? Did you touch?

Take the past and cut off its head,
you need no knife, you need no bread.

In the ivory of the Seven Towers,

be glad there's wood to burn
and a bed to rest your head.

Monument on a Mountaintop

for Endre Ady

This is a glass mountain.
Devils slide up and down its slopes.
This mound was built long ago
with the rinds of ruined souls.
And at midnight the mountain sings
to the dark world.

Hi-lee-ho, he died!…Oh, he died!…
Long silence.

The mountain flames, starts to dance,
something grave climbs to the top and stops,
high up there it stops. Lies down.
A pale spirit peels off from its face.
The mountain crystallizes into stairs.
You can see far from the top
and even farther from the shrine.

Who dares to look? These timid men?
Nothing but silence.
And the mountain roars. Shines.

Medallions

1
I was an elephant, pious and poor,
drank of waters wise and cool,
stood on a hill and with my trunk
caressed the moon and the sun,

and I lifted to their faces
flint, trees, snakes, dung beetles,
and now my soul: heaven disappears.
I fan myself with monstrous ears—

2
Dust crawls on dew drops,
arms hide holes in overalls,
the swineherd sobs, strokes
a piglet charmed into stone—

slow to blush, the sky smokes greenly,
chimes ripple over the dull lagoon,
frozen into sheets is the milk-white flower
on whose falling leaf hangs the world—

3
The leech-fisher shambles, shambles,
the bony swineherd marvels, marvels,
herons hover, hover over the pools,
fresh cowpie steams, cools—

a tired apple droops over my head,
chewed to the core for a worm's eye view
through which some can see the world,
the poem as an apple blossom, a flower—

4
You ought to be milk foam,
a murmur in the still night,
maybe a knife under rusty water,
maybe a loose, rolling button—

a servant girl's tears fall into dough,
don't look for kisses
when there's fire in the house,
pick up your feet, find your way home—
smoldering eyes will light the way—

5
A pig with knuckles of jasper
sits on a god carved from alabaster.
Hey, velvet shroud, thou art milk foam.
I will die a bard with a massive beard.

And if my heavenly skin cramps into folds,
the fat of my stomach will curdle into rolls.
They will swarm like white maggots,
to glisten like so many stars.

6
It's my fate
the green lizard seeks.
Wheat rustles, casts about seeds,
a stone drops, the lake takes me in.
The lake, the sky, and the grave.

War prophesying dawns
reel about my nodding head,
fleeting days and trembling stars
feverish with the world's dead.

7
On the threshold is a steel-wool bucket—
love the girl who sweeps barefooted.
Dirty water evaporates,
the scum dries where
she rolled up her sleeves—

I am warping into tiny bubbles.
Free and ringing they burst
over water like sea horses
over the glittering teeth of staircases—

8
A lawyer petrifies into amber,
squats and stares in black tails,
probes his envious cover, pets, blesses
the light, the wind, the haze—

A rose runs in here as I rot,
cool herons pick my flesh to flakes,
I am the oozing warmth of autumn nights
lest old men break out in gooseflesh—

9
I share a solitary bed with a friend.
There will be no lily withering here.
I have no Gattling gun, stone or arrow,
though I'd like to kill like anyone else.

And the beans simmer and hiss.
Your sauce-colored eyes see
my blathering jowls rolling in a fever.
The damned swallows keep feeding me
insects—

10
Curl up, my beard, crackle, sizzle,
fork and harrow the fields—
above the sky, below the clouds
where an unclaimed kiss is still afloat,

till its cool magic is brought to rest
in my beard whose red rivulets
trickle from the steam of good vintage.

11
Twenty-three kings
wear crowns of jasper
and eat honeydew melons,
a new moon shines in their left hand.

Twenty-three young men walk in a swagger,
wear gawky hats
and slurp watermelon,
a new sun shines in their right hand.

12
The black one has a flattened nose,
the yellow wears a halo of blue,
the red man's skin is burnt the most,
the white man is a flailing ghost—

Paris

A patron never rises in the morning.
In Paris Jeanettes are Berthas.
A man can buy cooked spinach
or burning candles at the barbershop.
Sixty naked women sing to heaven
down the St. Michel and Notre Dame:
it's cold inside, and for five francs
you can see me from above.
The Eiffel Tower tilts during the night
and nestles under quilted fog.
A policeman lets
you kiss him if you're a girl,
and there are no seats on the toilets.

Stones

Don't be angry with me, ancient stones,
because I step on you. I'm better
at stomping on headstones and bones.
I'm talking to you, old brothers.
Something heavier tramples me under,
walking on headstones, on aged haunches,
it doesn't speak, except through omens:
O mute ones, is it you?
And are these your sage words
I can't understand?

Why are there stones and no buildings?
Doesn't prayer or hallelujah help?
Or faith? Or mortar, for Christ's sake?
We fell, scattered into a million pieces
like adobe in the rain.
And where's the strong, rock-solid man
who knows of no pain?
It's unbearable like this,
lying in the street,
and no one will build us into cities
or granite mountains, though when young
we were lapping hills
where peace and brotherhood lived.

Insolence and bombs broke us apart.
Dissolved into blood and miserable tears,
a hundred succoring brains smolder like lime

that we may grow into sunlit cities.
Because our only concern
are the stones lying in the street,
trampled in the mire and dust,
longing to be a temple's towering dome!

Everything Is Old

Everything is old here. The ancient storm
leans on lightning's crooked shoulder
and whistles at the thorn-whiskered rose.
They hobble on bad feet.

Everything is old. The revolution
squats, coughing on sharp
scattered stones, a coin shines
in his bony hand: my favorite song.

Why isn't my hand transparent-old,
so that, touching a wrinkle on my face,
it would fall into my lap? They would
believe: tears roll from my eyes.

O my youth! My saintly lust!
Fish swarm in the net of twilight,
frog spawn curdles in the dust.

My Net

I'm running out of hair and bread,
    my fountain pen is dead.
My uncle the fisherman is dead.
True but sad.

I cast my network of nerves
like a fisherman's net
hoping to catch silver dreams
    and a little meat to go with it.

I think it's torn,
this net of mine.
I patch it up and hang it out to dry.
Then I take a closer look:

The frozen net sparkles
in the sky—
its icy knots the stars.

Leaves on a Tree

The leaves on the tree
flutter slowly.
They are curled, yellow,
    and withered with age.

A noiseless bird
flits up and down,
as if the tree
were a cage.

My heart is a bird
whose wings flutter
against my cage,
    and silence skips
      from rib to rib.

If only I could soar.
If only I could dance. My cage
trembles, my heart pounds,
skips and—oh—the silence!

Diamonds

Psalms are forever.

We stand on a diamond mountain,
our pockets full of pebbles.
And forgetting we were angels,
we stuffed our wings into fat quilts.
Pleas for mercy shored up our strength
and stones wore holes under our knees,
a star frozen in each breast.

Yes. Yes.
The sailors have foundered:
Meek oarsmen paddle toward God,
even the old ones
who sit on the simple wharf
and preach patience
to the ephemeral fish.

Yes. Yes.
Let's not forget, my friends,
we row with our fists instead of oars!
Everything has to be stroked lovingly,
the frogs as well as the wolves.

We stand on a diamond mountain,
harsh snow, cover our trespasses,
heavenly gossamer, loosen our tongues
into—oh—infinite crystals!

Yellow Grass

Yellow grass spears through the sand,
bony old woman, this wind:
the puddle is a strange brute,
the sea calm, willing to chat.

I hum my silent inventory:
a home that might as well be
a coat for sale,
dusk dissolving into dunes—
I have no words to go on.

Time glistens like coral:
Grass, trees, house,
a woman's sigh fuses into
rushing currents of sky.

Look

The sun's flaming train
rushes past melancholy doorways.

Go, your footprints
no longer hurt.

Silence.
Only a splash,
I give back my fat fish to the river,
a whisper,
I give back my frail bird to the field.
Just go.
The flower hides
withering leaves.

Look,
night
falls.

Soapy Water

Huddled between bricks
in the chilly courtyard,
cautiously dissolving
into nooks and crannies,

soapy water surges forward, stops.
Here and there its little blue head,
its almost invisible
feeler trembles

as it surveys each obstacle.
Like a captive it runs about
till death overtakes it
and passes it by.

The twitching skin
shakes its foamy mane. Yellow light
glows on a blue-green body

night's ashen fingers can't find.
It will not be. But as it trembles,
its slight shiver passes through me—

the intrusion of thought.

I would fly. And this branch would fly.
The house. The hay. The cloud.
All things linking this world.

Sorrow

I came here into the forest.
The leaves rustle like handbills,
the silence of the earth

lies dully, arms and limbs
reaching out for power.
A dry branch
falls on my head.
It hurts only for a moment,
almost gnashing,
not only for a moment,
it's just

that a rabid dog attacked me
and I came out to gather
what strength I had left.
Like an old woman, the sorrow.

Teardrops?
An ant drank of it
and saw his face.
It will not work anymore.

I May Just Vanish

I may just vanish suddenly
like a scent trail in the woods.
I wasted just about everything.
And more.

I sickened my young body,
curing it in a smoke house.
It stings my eyes to think
what I've become.

The sun
baked my green years,
and I got lost in a foreign war.
I'm a shell-shocked repentant
who should've waited longer,
maybe ten years or even more.

My defiance could not understand
a mother's voice, a mother's hand.
I was orphaned, grew more defiant,
played dumb or tormented my mentor.

My wild green freedom
could not last forever.

I had to learn to listen
to the sound of dry leaves
whispering in the trees.

The Sky Is Ablaze

The sky is ablaze. Frost spreads
stars on the tips of branches.
The aspen weeps. Fishermen
cast silent shadows in the water.

Their stiff boots touch the shore,
silt dissolves softly under soles.
Fish bodies glitter in the light,
the net rattles in the shallows.

A bulldog pike's dark body
lies like a shadow
on the carp's belly, its bruised
lips gaping and snapping
at the foam.

Consciousness

1
Dawn sifts earth from sky
and at her soft cry
all the insects and children
swirl into sunlight;
not a drop of dampness,
only the brilliant lightness!
Last night the leaves lit
the trees like butterflies.

2
I have seen
blue, red, yellow in dreams
and felt the order of things—
not one stone out of kilter.
Muted light leaks into joints,
dreams and steel become the one
and only order. The moon rises
by day and by night the sun.

3
Living only on bread
I reach for something
more certain than dice
among the idle and the frivolous.
Roast beef does not rub
against my mouth or a child
against my heart. Lips
cannot catch them,

or the cat the mouse
both inside and out.

4
Worlds lie on one another
like a pile of wood,
squeezing, pressing,
each other's being.
What-cannot-be always
sprouts branches,
what-will-be are the flowers,
what-is smashes into pieces.

5
Like a stump of silence
I lean against the wood
in the freight yard;
gray weed touches my mouth,
raw, oddly sweet.
Still as a corpse, I follow
the watchman's moods:
his shadow flickers
on wet coal in the boxcar.

6
The torment inside
cries out for redemption.
The earth is a wound that festers
and singes, and the fever is the soul,
a slave of rebellion—
free only when we build a house

where the landlord has no dominion.

7
I looked beyond the night
at the cog-wheel of heaven and saw
in the smog of my dream
threads of braiding cables
out of which the loom
of the past weaves its law,
only to burst at the seams.

8
Silence cocks its ear. Strikes one.
We may still reclaim our youth,
imagine a little freedom
between prison walls—the stars
in the Milky Way are shining bars.

9
I heard the thunder of iron.
I heard the laughter of rain.
I saw the ages rent asunder,
forgetting mere images.
Broken under all this weight
all we can do is love—
lest we forge weapons of rage?

Consciousness.

10
A whole man

has no mother, no father in his heart.
He knows that life
was given in addition to death,
and he must give it back
any moment—like the finder his find.
He is no God and no priest.

11
But I have seen happiness.
It was soft and blond and 300 lbs.
Its curly smile wobbled in the pen.
It lay in a warm puddle,
squinting, snorting. The light
was tickling its down.

12
I live near the tracks
for what it's worth.
Trains come and go
with glittering windows,
rush of days in the eternal night.
The poet leans on his elbows,
standing in the flitting light
of passing berths,
and listens.

Smoke

A smoke wisp blooms in front of the moon,
silver sashes tie, unbind, and bow.
Cool air seeps through the cloud.

I have suffered till I'm worn.
I fly off like everyday troubles—
cool air seeps through the cloud.

I fly off, but then a feverish tremor
for life rocks the world
and seeps through the cool air.

Bitter

O radioactivity! I'm reading, eating a
watermelon
    and I know
    the world changes only within us.
I'm only a colored rattle, do you hear me?
My face
    is transparent, behind it flowers soar,
    popped from electronic waves.
A humanist century tears me from my love,
    oh flicked-off sorrow.
Burn the orphanages.
Lambs are sheep, and I'm an ass,
    not even the shadow of a shepherd.
If I close my eyes airplanes crash, and those too
    that wing from me daily.
Glittering dust, halt your gilded motors because
    she will sweep you out in the morning.
O woman, my lover's tears can drive
    those ancient turbines
and it's a shame,
but let this whistling apprentice grinder live.
He doesn't even know the sky
    has sailed into his wallet.

I Threw It

I threw myself here while the blind knock
about our hearts. Our intentions
are one with radium,
tomorrow we'll be Jehovahs
making ourselves anew.
Yes, this is love and the song of the lyre,
whose chords we stretch till the water washes
our ankles. A wave-length
measures my height,
and I call the giddy solar system "kisses"—
prayers smiling under black tresses.
Hours wither into oppressive dreams
but a violet garden swims inches above cities.
A train rushes toward them and a slim tower
cries to them in the shadow of tears.
Lyrics wax classical in poets' eyes,
and there's no one to pour fresh water
to mourn their innocent lives.

The Ant

The ant fell asleep among the eggs.
Wind, try not to blow her eggs away!
Maybe it doesn't matter either way.
Resting her tired head on a shell,
she sleeps with her shadow.

We could prod her with a straw.
But it's better if we start for home,
the sky is overcast—

An ant fell asleep among her eggs
and—oops—a drop just fell on my hand.

Rain

it rains it rains
dust curdles on bodies

thunder-ring
can you hear them pounding
on our hearts?

naked
to run to run
toward the forest with open arms

rain rain
you hold out your tiny finger
for the blasting ring

the wind had brought it
the wind

from laughing girls
who let their hair down long

over the dry leaves
heartlessly
through the spaces between the trees.

I'm Leaving Everything

God must've really loathed
to spit such an ugly planet—
And he said it was good?
I'm leaving everything

by this damned electric fence.
I will lie down
in the pasture of my heart.
I will be my own flock
in a sheepfold of one.

I used to think I was wicked,
that time would mow me down,
and I exalted all others
because they did not see
yet believed in miracles.

If I was wicked, it was because of this.
I saw myself for a split second
standing in the sun. *In the sun*.
My ribs pounded. My head swam
in my blood. The sun said
I was dead. The only one
to take a stand against the sun.

The wind squalled. Took my heart
and the last drop of blood
and heaved them across the heavens.
A comet with its tail

falling from the sky…

I'm leaving everything.
The earth can burn for all I care.
Sleep comes easily
on the bed of my heart.
My grin is wide and white,
a single whitecap in the vast
green of the sea.

Perched on Nothing's Branch

I finally arrive
at the sand's wet edge,
look around, shrug

that I am where I am,
staring at the end.
A silver ax strokes
summer leaves. Playfully.

I'm perched solidly
on nothing's branch.
The small body shivers
to receive heaven.

Iron-colored.

Cool shiny dynamos revolve
in the quiet revolution of stars.
Words barely spark from clenched teeth.

The past tumbles
stone-like through space,
blue time floating off
without a sound. A blade
flashes, my hair—

My mustache is a full
caterpillar drooping
down my numb mouth,

my heart aches, words are cold.
There's no one out here
to hear—

FIVE
At the Sand's Wet Edge

Bathing in the Sea

Green sunshine dances on the foam.
My naked body is buoyant in the sea.

I swim to the edge of the horizon
and lay spread-eagle with my eyes closed,
soaking in the streaks of sky that swaddle
me in lace.
    So much grace. So much grace.
I rock in my cradle.

Then something happens. An ancient chill
washes over me, terror surges
from an animal heart that wails until
a wave smacks it across the mouth.

Then a wild roar. It does not let up. More
terrible than a herd of giant lizards.
It was the sea and me having it out,

forgetting how little life is worth.

Shadows

Shadows lengthen,
stars appear in the distance.
Flames singe the air.
We are forever fixed
like the constellations.
Your absence
is a black hole
that sucks me in.

Night swells like the sea,
smelling of green pestilence
the kind that chokes
off your last breath.

Sink your net into *my* abyss,
look into my marble eyes,
and raise me from the dead
with your life-saving kiss.

Longing Under the Moon

It's good to go into the night
alone under the moon;
roam the streets and drink in
the gloom of this spring evening.

The moon sleeps, not a breeze,
flowers open to be forgotten,
roses ignite the dark
on prickly stems,
a tapestry of pestilence.

Secret music of dying linden
(the soul's eternal fragrance).
This cool night is in mourning.
It is spring. Someone is leaving.

I've wandered off course. Hidden
yet familiar. Nobody comes here.
Nobody. This is my garden of agony.
My great sin is that I dared.

Dared to look and wander
into the cool night air,
eye to eye with my despair.

Silent night, holy night,
I drink you in.

The Bellman of the Lake's Tower

Just like a man who's broke
I mixed beet-leaves with my tobacco
for which my pipe thanked me
as it sucked in, coughed,
and looked after its blue
son of a smoke,
who got as far as the lake's tower
where soulful violas, still cloudy,
composed and resolved themselves
into poetry:
it was about virgin boys and the lake,
and hairs of gold.
Wake up and look how tall you've grown—
why even the man at the store says
your mother will be buying you
long pants
soon.
And there
in the tower,
despite the prohibition against alcohol,
the bellman who hanged himself
is dangling in his long pants.

Hearsay

I was born with a knife in my hand—
they say this is just poetry.
Trust me: a knife wasn't enough,
so I reached for a pen.
    I was born a man,

too passionate for his own good,
but an infant just the same.
They say I love everything,
like putting my head in your lap.
Oh, it's just a game.
    Or is it?

I don't remember, I don't forget.
    "Is it possible?" they say.
Whatever I drop stays where it lands,
what I leave behind,
you are meant to find.

The earth covers my body,
the sea washes over me.
I will die, I heard them say.

Hearsay?

My Funeral

A sallow priest cracks a smile
and praises an indifferent God.
Bored wasps drone on the road.
Mourners are paid to follow.

A frightened brown-eyed girl
presses her nose against the hearse,
her father taps her on the ass
with the stem of his pipe.

The smell of dung on the grass,
red dawn a smudge between the trees,
a branch snaps, a grasshopper leaps
into a spider-web of uneasy dreams.

Memories are dim.
My informer
slinks to my grave.

And I can't sic my dog on him.

Balatonszárszó

1
Autumn howls,
rips green into foam.
Small storms play hide and seek,
flies are dying by the window.

The landscape whirls and delights
in the bright spaces of silence.
Yellow trees stand on one foot
and blink at the sun.

Snatched into the current
I long for a bed.
I have packed away my everyday
clothes and dress somberly
in finer linen.

2
The night reels in large irritable waves,
water gurgles underneath the boat.
It feels lovely and melancholy in your lap.

Autumn is cold.
People are always sad when they learn
to tremble again. Cool shadows start
the old ones coughing.

3
Je n'ai point de thème,
excepté que je t'aime—

That is all I could write
as I kept falling asleep…
we touched each other.

She wore glasses on her nose
and looked at me from under them.

I pressed her to me
and she closed her eyes under her glasses.
We were always disturbed.

The train left.

But I didn't linger for long.
It rained and I went home.

She left me a hundred grams of tobacco
for cigarettes.

No dreams, only sleep.
We will not see each other again.

On Glasses

Glasses are fresh clean plants:
they glitter, dew cleaves to them;
if we stare at them long enough
they will ring out softly.
Glasses bloom in the hearts of springs
but the glassmakers are ignorant
of their secret.
Men and women keep mistaking
each other's glasses.

I had mixed them up myself once
and since then no glass of water
has been sweet enough,
though a bird dying of thirst will
notice the many shiny glasses
beyond the clouds.

Summoning the Lion

I bit down hard on a cigar,
a switchblade slit open my arm,
I was bathed by the mother of storms,
a green fly buzzed into my open mouth,
a wrinkled granny slept on my couch,
the poor thing had such lovely dreams.

Coughing up blood brought me love,
but I don't spit on the virgin snow.
No.
I may have been a raging beast:
"Let's wake the dead," I may have said.
"Make him speak, make him laugh."
I may have had a drink or two,
gnawed on a few pig knuckles,
shook hands with my left foot,
plucked a song on my only tooth.

I gave up the ghost on all religions,
the clothes on me are a gentleman's,
let the sissy come and find me,
my heart is bitter, lean and mean.

I look into the mirror.
I summon the lion—

His shaggy mane can
shine my shoes;
he can pet me,

claw out my gaping throat,
lick my face with my eyes closed.
he can lie on my bed
and roar and roar that I'm dead.

A Transparent Lion

A transparent lion lives between black walls,
I wear a pressed suit in my heart
when I speak to you,
I mustn't think of you before my work is done.

You're dancing.

I haven't had any bread and will live a long life,
it's been five weeks, I don't know where you are.
Time runs off on wooden legs
and the streets are buried in snow.
I wonder if anyone could love you.
Mute Negroes play chess. Long silences.

The Smoke

Factory smoke
spirals toward heaven,
silver sparks braid
ashes in the air.

She kneads clenched fingers,
and heals the sorrow and the tears.
The sorrow and the tears.
But if it please her
she can burn and kill.

She falls upon the wailing wall,
shrouds an arm,

and offering a valiant prayer,
in her darkness, in her pride,
she ascends almost to God
somewhere.

It's Only the Sea

The blue light between your breasts,
a tightrope in an acrobat's dream.

A cloud floats off and you float off.
I follow clouds searching for you,
I breathe in deep, still waters.
Sturdy pine cones fall from my limbs.
The tallest grasses sprout on the hill,
lovely, green fires glow in their hearts.
The insects are too tired
to find their way home.
Come evening, the Lord God will come.
He will come with open arms.
I'm not tired anymore.

It's only the sea at my door.

Freight Trains

back up in the distance.
Dull, clanking links.
Manacles on silence.

Free of the earth,
the moon off
without much effort.

Broken stones
rest on their shadows,
they glitter
only for their glory,
fitting like never before.

Is this deep night
only a splinter
of a deeper dark?

Hail of iron ore
burns the skin
to the pore.

A hiss.

One bed, one shadow.
Would you still keep vigil
on a night like this?

A Summer Afternoon

Chatter of clippers. A woman
    is trimming the lawn,
then stops. Even from behind
    you can see her yawn.

The radio drones. Wings
    on the glass.
A gust of wind
across the grass.

Time stands still
    with nothing to do but pass.
Flowers tremble
on the windowsill.

It's been a while. I don't know
if I'm sleeping or working or both.
Before me spreads
    a lovely white tablecloth.

The sky here lights up
    like homespun linen;
it glistens the wet strawberries
    in the bowl.

I am happy. She sits near me
    and sews while I listen
for a freight train's distant roar.

Autumn Dusk

Autumn's brown dusk
flakes quietly
on the freezing snow.

I feel your warm arm,
your lovely neck nestles
against my shoulder.
You are far away,
but my skin
remembers your lips.

The cold howls,
cutting into my face—
I can't lay it in your warm lap.

You are so far away.
Twilight is sad.
Snow falls in great, gentle flakes.
Something like sorrow.

Loneliness

May a bug crawl on your open eye.
And green mold grow on your breast.
I have you to thank for this loneliness.
Grind your teeth down, eat your tongue.

Your face can blow away like sand.
When you want me near,
you'll feel an empty lap,
dry weeds instead of my hair.

Take a good look at what you are.
Nothing. Maybe one, gaping,
terrible longing.
You have made a beast of me.

Who are you sleeping with now?
If you bear a child, he can ride
a merry-go-round on a fat-bellied,
slithering crocodile.

I'm on my bed,
not moving a cell in my body.
I watch myself through your open eye.
Die! Die! I want you bad enough to die.

Drunk on the Tracks

A drunk is lying on the tracks,
clutching a bottle in his hand,
snoring as in the arms of his lover.
Night has swallowed up the day.

The wind tousles weeds into his hair,
wraps him in godly mist so he doesn't stir,
except for a chest that heaves strangely.

Like a rail-tie, the hardness of his fist.
He can sleep here as on his mother's lap.
His clothes are rags, he's a young man.

No room for the sun, the sky is ashes.
It's only a drunk lying on the tracks,
and from far away, the roar of the earth.

Nothing

Nothing, nothing, nothing, nothing, nothing.
Let it be, so it won't be,
let it be, so it won't be—let us say: Edith.
Small invisible yellow chickens
peck at the stars.

Maybe it's dawn and Budapest is burning.
Warm paint melting
on a giant girl's sweating face.
Cars rumble, shutters rattle,
the sea thunders, people swarm.

That rude house on the corner makes me
angry—
it's like acne on a child's face.

Or is this an unfamiliar morning,
or a foreign railway station
where I've come?

I have no luggage.
There's something I forgot—maybe if I remember.
One: nothing.
Two: nothing.
Three: nothing.
Sounds peculiar as the rail station
where there's nothing at all.

Weary Man

Over the fields somber peasants start
silently home.
We lie next to each other, the river and I.
Limp grass sleeps beneath my heart.

The river is quiet, ushers great peace,
all my troubles dissolve into vapor.
I am no longer Hungarian or man
or child or anyone's brother—
only the weary lie here.

Night passes out the silence.
I am a slice of its warm bread.
Heaven sleeps now, and the stars
rest on my forehead
and on the quiet river.

Dew

A raspberry bush squats,
cradles the greasy paper
stirring in her arms.

The earth is soft, the night
delicate as a pearl.
Thick, twisting branches
braid softly. Mountain mists
tremble to my song.

I have worked all day
humming like the fields.
How easy heaven can be!
My workshop is dark now.

I am tired or simply good.
I shimmer like the grass.
Like the stars.

About Attila József

(in his own words)

I was born in 1905 in Budapest; my religion is Greek Orthodox. My father, the late Áron József, left the country when I was three years old, and through the efforts of the Children's Protective Agency I was made to live with foster parents at Öcsöd. I lived there until I was seven, already working, as a swineherd, along with the other poor children. When I was seven years old my mother, the late Borbála Pöcze, brought me back to Budapest and enrolled me in the second grade. My mother provided for me and my two sisters by taking in washing and housework. Working at different houses, she was gone from morning till night. Left without parental supervision, I started skipping school, getting into trouble. It was in a third grade reader that I found some interesting stories about Attila the Hun, so I threw myself into reading. The stories about Attila fascinated me all the more because my name was Attila. My foster parents at Öcsöd had insisted on calling me Steve. They said there was no such Christian name as Attila. I was astounded. The very existence of my being was called into question. I believe that it was this experience which made me into a thinking person, one who regards the opinions of others but examines them carefully in his own mind, one who can answer to the name of Steve until it is proven what he had known all along—that his name is Attila.

I was nine when the world war broke out. Our situation worsened. I had to stand in food lines, sometimes from nine in the evening until seven thirty in the morning, only to be told when it got to be my turn that they were out of lard. I helped my mother as best I could. I sold water at the Világ movie theatre. I stole coal and lumber from the Ferencváros station to have something to heat with. I made pinwheels from colored paper and sold them to children who were better off. I carried baskets, bags, packages in the shoppers' market, etc. In the summer of 1918 King Károly's Children's Fund sent me to a camp in Abbázia. My mother was already suffering from a tumor of the uterus, and on my own I asked for assistance from the Children's Protective Agency, and for a brief time they sent me to Monor. Once I was back in Budapest I sold newspapers, postage stamps, food stamps, blue and white banknotes, like a little banker. During the Rumanian occupation I worked as a bread boy at the Café Emke. During this time I was attending secondary school, after five years of elementary.

My mother died in 1919 during Christmas. My brother-in-law, the late Dr. Ödön Makai, was appointed my legal guardian. I spent the spring and the summer working on the tugboats *Vihar*, *Török*, and *Tatár* of the Atlantic Shipping Company while preparing for special secondary school examinations as a private student. After this, my guardian and Dr. Sándor Giesswein sent me to a seminary at Nyergesújfalu so I could begin my training for the Salesian Order. I spent only two weeks there; I am, after all, Greek Orthodox, not Roman Catholic. From here I went to Demke, a boarding school that, after a short time, offered me free tuition. In the summers I earned my room and board by tutoring students around Mezőhegyes. I finished my sixth year of secondary school with honors, despite an attempted suicide, probably triggered by adolescence and the problems of transition; then, as before, no one stood by me as a friend. My first poems appeared around this time. I was seventeen when *Nyugat* published some of my poems. They thought I was a child prodigy when I was just an orphan.

After my sixth year, I left the boarding school because I was bored and alone: I had stopped studying and going to lectures but I still knew my lessons—as my superior grade reports attest. I went to Kiszombor where I did some tutoring and worked in a corn field as watchman and farmhand. On the advice of two kindly teachers of mine I decided to finish my last two years of study and graduate. As it turned out I passed all my examinations and graduated a year ahead of my former classmates. I had only three months in which to prepare and that is why I received only a "good" for the seventh grade and a "satisfactory" for the eighth. My final examination grades were actually better: I received a grade of satisfactory only in Hungarian and History. It was around this same time that I was accused of blasphemy because of one of my poems. But I was acquitted.

Later I was a textbook salesman in Budapest, and during the economic inflation I clerked at the Mauthner private bank. Following the introduction of the Hintz system I joined the accounting department and soon after, and much to the annoyance of my senior colleagues, I was entrusted with supervising the currency values that were to be paid on account. My enthusiasm started to flag once I was assigned extra duties routinely performed by my senior colleagues who spent their time jeering at me about my poetry which was now appearing in periodicals. "I used to write poetry too when I was your age," they would laugh. Later the bank failed.

I made up my mind then to be a writer and to find a position closely connected with literature. I registered for courses in Hungarian and French literature and philosophy in the College of Arts at the University of Szeged. I attended 52 hours of lectures and seminars, but at least now I could eat regularly. I was very proud when one of the professors, Lajos Dézsi, nominated me to undertake independent research. My hopes were dashed, however, when another professor, Antal Horger, my examiner in Hungarian Literature, called me in before two witnesses. I still remember their names, they are teachers now. Professor Horger made a statement to the effect that I was not to be trusted with the education of the future generation because of the kind of poetry I wrote. Here the professor held up a copy of the periodical *Szeged* where my poem, "Tiszta szivvel" ("With all My Heart"), was published. You talk about the irony of fate. This poem of mine got to be quite famous. Seven articles have been written on the poem since: Lajos Hatvany spoke of it as not only the document of the postwar generation but of "future generations" as well; and writing in *Nyugat* Ignotus said that he "fondled it, caressed it, cherished it in his soul, murmuring, humming" this "wonderful" poem; it was this poem which he placed in his *Ars Poetica* as the model of the new poetry.

The following year—I was twenty then—I went to Vienna, enrolled at the University, sold newspapers in front of the Rathaus Keller and cleaned the quarters of the Vienna Hungarian Academy. Once Antal Lábán, the director, heard about me, he put an end to all this, provided for meals at the Vienna Hungarian Academy, and found me pupils: I tutored the two sons of Zoltán Hajdu, director of the Anglo-Austrian Bank. From a terrible slum in Vienna, where for four months I had no sheets with which to cover myself, I went straight to the Hatvany castle as guest. The lady of the house, Mrs. Albert Hirsch, gave me travelling expenses to go to Paris at the end of the summer. There I enrolled at the Sorbonne. I spent the next summer in southern France in a fishing village.

After that I returned to Budapest. I completed two semesters at the University. I didn't take my teacher's examination because, thinking back on Antal Horger's threats, I didn't feel I could secure a position. Once the Foreign Trade Institute was founded I was hired there to handle French correspondence. My former supervisor, Mr. Sándor Kóródi, will be happy to supply you with a reference. But then I suffered a series of unexpected setbacks that, no matter how life had toughened me, made it unbearable for me to go on. The OTI Health Service referred me to a sanitarium for neurasthenia. I resigned my job to avoid being a burden on the young institute. I live now solely from my writing. I am editor of *Szép szó,* a literary and critical periodical. Other than my native Hungarian, I write and read French and German, can write Hungarian and French business correspondence, and consider myself a good typist. I used to know shorthand—all I need is a month's practice. I am familiar with printing techniques, I can express myself clearly. I consider myself honest and, I believe, perceptive, and when it comes to work I am sturdy by nature.

Note: Attila József wrote this "Curriculum Vitae" as part of a job application in February, 1937, ten months before he threw himself under the wheels of a freight train.

About the Translator

PETER HARGITAI is the author of twelve books, among them his volume of poems, *Mother Tongue: A Broken Hungarian Love Song*. His selection of the poems of Attila József in *Perched on Nothing's Branch* garnered for him the Academy of American Poets Landon Translation Award and a listing among world classics in Harold Bloom's *The Western Canon*. His versions are not just translations. They are re-creations. As a poet he is able to inject himself into the heart of the poems. By conveying the spirit of each poem, he is able to avoid banal mirror translations, jingly rhymes and archaic cadences, allowing the originals to thrive in contemporary English as the great poems that they are in their original Hungarian. For his translation of Antal Szerb's novel *The Traveler*, he was awarded the Füst Milán Prize from the Hungarian Academy of Sciences; and for his steadfast commitment to translating, publishing, and teaching Hungarian literature in a world language, he was awarded the Pro Cultura Hungarica Medal from the Republic of Hungary. Professor Hargitai is on the English faculty at Florida International University in Miami and a member of the Hungarian Writers' Association in Budapest.

978-0-595-35614-0
0-595-35614-1

Printed in Great Britain
by Amazon